Cro... Flower Fairy Dolls

7 Adorable Amigurumi Flower Doll Crochet Patterns

7 Adorable Amigurumi Flower Fairy Doll Crochet Patterns - Most Pretty Amigurumi Flower Doll Crochet Patterns.

Hi guys! If you're got in your mind that you want to make something extra special for a little girl doll in your life, then why not look at this list of 7 Amigurumi Flower Fairy Doll Crochet Patterns? Ripe with potential for color combinations and spring appeal with cornflowers, summer with brilliant roses, autumn with chrysanthemums, winter with clear snowflakes, any of these adorable crochet flower dolls would be a treasured gift for a long time to come! These stylish amigurumi flower dolls will be adorable, magical, and fanciful. These are also great choices for little girls who love flowers and fairy gardening! When you want to keep it simple, you can enjoy a few that make the flower literally part of the doll! With a doll-shaped crochet pattern combined with a floral skirt as well as a neat bun or long curly hairstyle, it creates a beautiful fairy doll, for those that want to keep it a little more simple, these are great! These are great for little ones to play with and snuggle with during naptime. (custom size)

5

12

17

24

32

39

46

A breakdown of what yarn is used for on certain hooks

USA	Purpose	Hook Size(mm)
Lace	This is super light weight yarn and is ideal for intricate projects.For this yarn it is best to use small needles and hooks	0.75-3.0mm
Sock/ Fingering	This yarn is great for baby clothing including toys.	2.25-3.5mm
Fingering/Sports	This yarn is also suitable baby clothing and lighter weight knits	2.5 – 3.5mm
Light Worsted	Also known as "DK". This is the most popular choice of yarn.This is a very versatile yarn as it is cost effective and quick to knit.	3.5-4.5mm
Worsted	This is also a quick yarn to knit with and is ideal for the following; sweaters, cardigans.	5.5mm-6.5mm
Chunky	This is great for knitting with larger needles and is perfect for rugs	6.5mm-9.0mm
Bulky	This is yarn is thick and it easy and quick to finish your project.	9.0mm & above
Jumbo	This yarn is great for beginners as it is thick and chunky and mistakes will be noticed quickly.	15mm and above

Helpful Notes:

◆ This is a guide, so please always check the pattern or yarn instructions. to choose the right type of yarn and crochet hook

◆ Always check tension as this could make a huge difference.

◆ Change the hook to a smaller size if there are signs of holes when crocheting the dolls

Ways To Modify a Crochet Pattern

Enlarge a Pattern

(If you are interested in designing mini dolls, then use the yarn and crochet hook I show you for each pattern below. If you prefer larger dolls, follow these instructions (make sure to keep the suitable yarn and crochet hook combination to create the perfect product to your liking.)

1. Use the Same Yarn but With a Larger Hook. (It is not recommended to use this method because the sample may have holes in it, although it is not too much larger than the old model)

2. Double-strand the Yarn and increase the hook size (sample size will increase markedly)

3. Increase the Height of Stitches. To increase the height of the stitches, I went to the next height stitch for all stitches – half double crochet to double crochet, double crochet to treble crochet, and treble crochet to double treble crochet.

4. Thicker Yarn (It creates a much larger end project and lets you play around with the textures of the project.)

Skills and abbreviations

(): repeat instructions between parentheses, as many times as directed

[]: number in [] at the end of the row indicates the number of stitches at round.

Mr-magic ring

Ch-chain

Slst-slip stitch

Sc-single crochet

Inc - single crochet increase - 2 single crochet in 1 stitch

Dec - single crochet invisible decrease - sc 2 stitch together

Hdc - half double crochet

Dc - double crochet

Blo - crochet through back loops only

Flo - crochet through front loops only

Rnd - Round

Snowflake Doll

Materials & Tools

Hook: 0,75mm and 0,9mm

Yarn: YarnArt Canarias

Yarn color: skin

I use needle felting for hair: brown color

Craft Wire 1.5mm

Glitter ribbon 1cm

Cotton Candy 40gram: white color

White thread

Cotton Stuffing

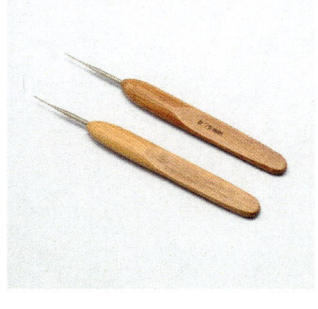

6194

Head

Skin color yarn

Rnd1. Mr 6sc   [6]

Rnd2. 6inc [12]

Rnd3. (sc, inc)*6 [18]

Rnd4. (2sc, ins)*6 [24]

Rnd5. (3sc, ins)*6 [30]

Rnd6. (4sc, ins)*6 [36]

Rnd7. (5sc, ins)*6 [42]

Rnd8. (20sc, ins)*2 [44]

Rnd9 – 18. 44sc [44]

Rnd19. (20sc, dec)*2 [42]

Rnd20. (4sc, dec)*7 [35]

Rnd21. (3sc, dec)*7 [28]

Rnd22. (2sc, dec)*7 [21]

Rnd23. (sc, dec)*7 [14]

Rnd24. (sc, dec)*4, 2sc [10]

Rnd25. Blo 10sc [10]

Rnd26 – 28. 10sc [10]

Arms*2

Skin color yarn

Rnd1. Mr 6sc   [6]

Rnd2. (2inc, sc)*2   [10]

Rnd3 – 4. 10SC   [10]

Rnd5. (sc, dec)*3, sc   [7]

Rnd6 – 19. 7sc   [7]

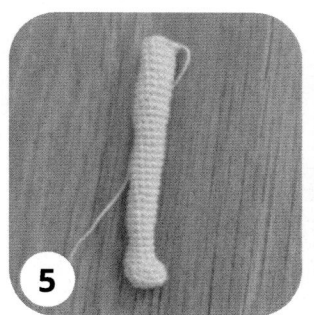
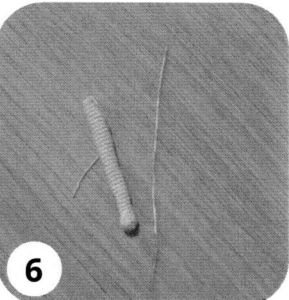
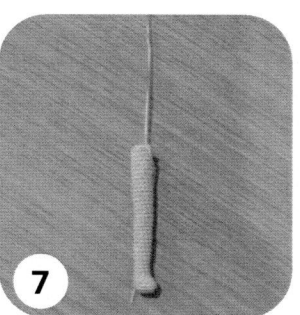

Legs*2
Skin color yarn

Rnd1. Ch5, turn: 3sc,3sc in 1st, 2sc, inc [10]

Rnd2. Inc, 2sc, 3inc, 2sc, 2inc [16]

Rnd3. Blo 16sc [16]

Rnd4. 3sc, 4dec, 5sc [12]

Rnd5. 2sc, 3dec, 4sc [9]

Rnd6 – 7. 9sc [9]

Rnd8. 8sc, inc [10]

Rnd9. 9sc, inc [11]

Rnd10 – 22. 11sc [11]

Rnd23. inc, 10sc [12]

Rnd24. inc, 11sc [13]

Rnd25 – 34. 13sc [13]

Rnd35. 4sc, inc, 8sc [14]

Put Craft Wire in 2 leg

Body
Skin color yarn

Rnd37. Join 2 in legs and body into one piece

Continue crocheting on the right leg

Rnd36: ch2, 14sc on left leg, 2sc on ch2, 14 sc on right leg, 2sc on ch2 [32]

Rnd38 – 40. (7sc, inc)*4 [36]

Rnd41. (4sc, dec)*6 [30]

Rnd42. 30sc [30]

Rnd43. Blo (3sc, dec)*6 [24]

Rnd44. (dec, 10sc)*2 [22]

Rnd45 – 52. 22sc [22]

Join 2 arms and body into one piece.

Rnd53. 6sc on body, 3sc on body and arm, 8sc on body, 3sc on body and arm, 2sc on body [22]

Rnd54. 4sc, dec (on body), 4sc (on arm), dec, 4sc. dec (on body), 4sc (on arm), dec (on body) [20]

Rnd55. sc, (dec,sc)*6, sc [16]

Rnd56. sc, 6dec, sc [8]

Rnd57 – 64. 8sc [8]

Put Craft Wire in 2 arms

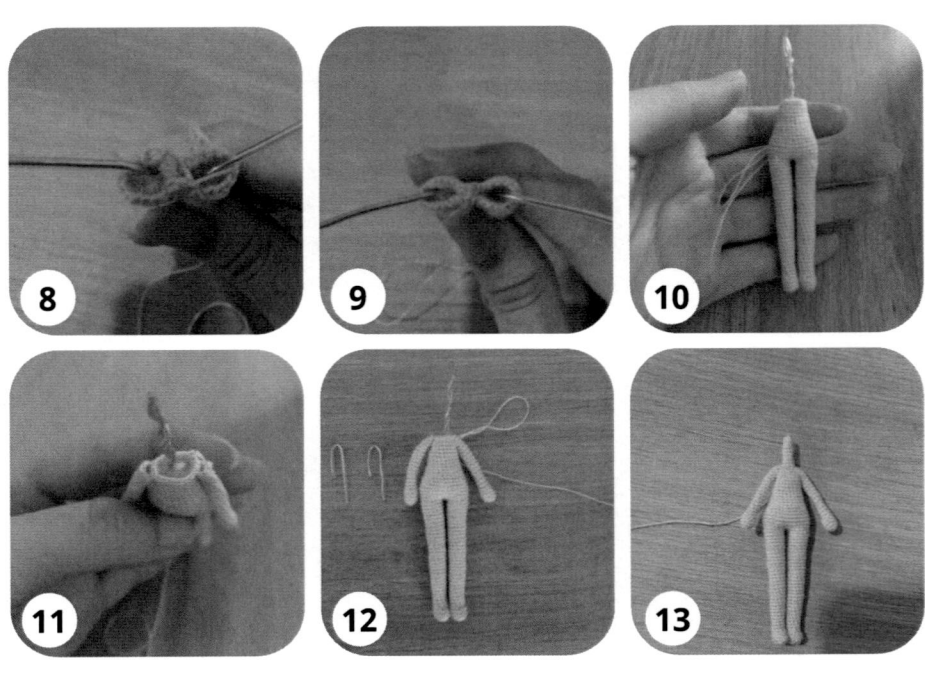

8

9

10

11

12

13

Dress

Use glitter ribbon to make the top
Use Cotton Candy - White color (*A strand of wool is twisted from three small threads, separate one small thread to crochet*)
Hook 0.9mm

Rnd1: 23ch, start in 2nd , 22dc [22]
Rnd2: (2dc in 1st)*22 [44]
Rnd3 – 4: 44dc [44]
Rnd5: (1dc, 2dc in 1st)*22 [66]
Rnd6 – 8: 66dc [66]
Rnd9: (2sc,2dc in 1st)*22 [88]
Rnd10 – 13: 88dc [88]

Flower

Rnd1. Mr 5sc
Rnd2. (2ch, 2dc, 2ch, slst)*5

Wings

Use felt fabric to cut into the shape of wings,
use glitter ribbon glue, trim neatly

Horns

Use 1.5mm Craft Wire to shape the horn, use white
thread to surround it

Hair

I use needle felting for hair

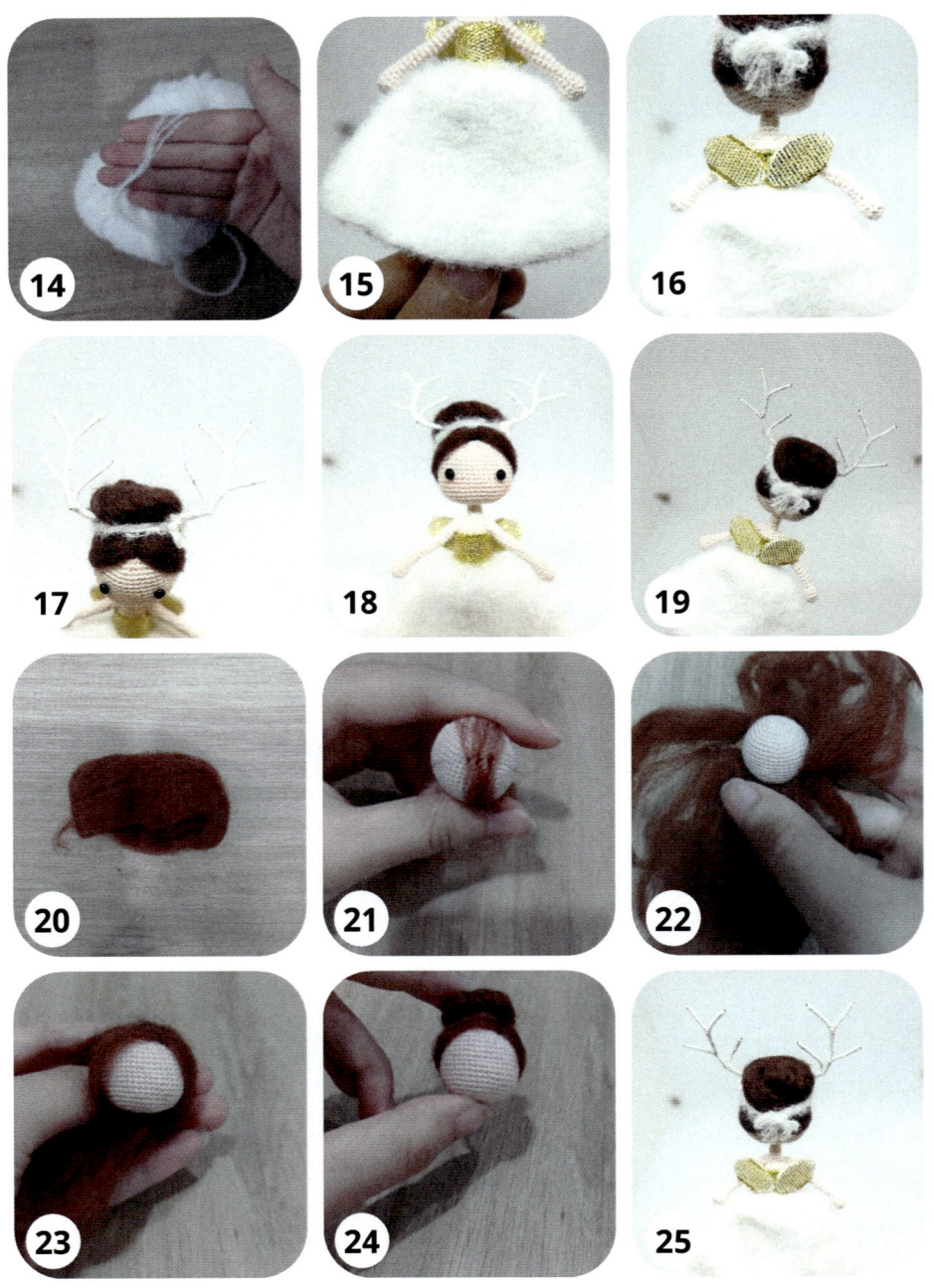

14

15

16

17

18

19

20

21

22

23

24

25

Cornflower
Mermaid Fairy Doll

Materials & Tools

Hook: 0,75mm

Yarn: YarnArt Canarias

Yarn color: blue, white, skin

I use needle felting for hair -Blue color

Craft Wire 1.5mm

Cotton Stuffing

Head

Skin color yarn

Rnd1. Mr 6sc   [6]

Rnd2. 6inc [12]

Rnd3. (sc, inc)*6 [18]

Rnd4. (2sc, ins)*6   [24]

Rnd5. (3sc, ins)*6 [30]

Rnd6. (4sc, ins)*6   [36]

Rnd7. (5sc, ins)*6 [42]

Rnd8. (20sc, ins)*2 [44]

Rnd9 – 18. 44sc [44]

Rnd19. (20sc, dec)*2 [42]

Rnd20. (4sc, dec)*7 [35]

Rnd21. (3sc, dec)*7 [28]

Rnd22. (2sc, dec)*7 [21]

Rnd23. (sc, dec)*7 [14]

Rnd24. (sc, dec)*4, 2sc [10]

Rnd25. Blo 10sc [10]

Rnd26 – 28. 10sc [10]

Arms*2

Skin color yarn

Rnd1. Mr 6sc   [6]

Rnd2. (2inc, sc)*2   [10]

Rnd3 – 4. 10SC   [10]

Rnd5. (sc, dec)*3, sc   [7]

Rnd6 – 19. 7sc   [7]

Body

Blue color yarn

Rnd1. Mr 6sc [6]

Rnd2. 6sc [6]

Rnd3. sc, inc, 2sc, inc, sc [8]

Rnd4. inc, 6sc, inc [10]

Rnd5. inc, 8sc, inc [12]

Rnd6. inc, 10sc, inc [14]

Rnd7. inc, 12sc, inc [16]

Rnd8. inc, 14sc, inc [18]

Rnd9. inc, 16sc, inc [20]

Rnd10. inc, 18sc, inc [22]

Rnd11. inc, 20sc, inc [24]

Rnd12. inc, 22sc, inc [26]

Rnd13. inc, 24sc, inc [28]

Rnd14. 28sc [28]

Rnd15. inc, 26sc, inc [30]

Rnd16. 30sc [30]

Rnd17. inc, 28sc, inc [32]

Rnd18 – 19. 32sc [32]

Rnd20. inc, 30sc, inc [34]

Rnd21 – 24. 34sc [34]

Rnd25. dec, 30sc, dec [32]

Rnd26. dec, 28sc, dec [30]

Rnd27. dec, 26sc, dec [28]

Rnd28 – 29 . 28sc [28]

Rnd30. (2sc, dec)*7 [21]

Change to skin color yarn

Rnd31. Blo 21sc [21]

Rnd32. 10sc, inc, 10sc [22]

Rnd33 – 38. 22sc   [22]

Join 2 arms and body into one piece.

Rnd39. 6sc on body, 3sc on body and arm, 8sc on body, 3sc on body and arm, 2sc on body, [22]

Rnd40. 4sc, dec (on body), 4sc (on arm), dec, 4sc. dec (on body), 4sc (on arm), dec (on body) [20]

Rnd41. sc, (dec,sc)*6, sc [16]

Rnd42. sc, 6dec, sc [8]

Rnd43 – 50. 8sc [8]

Use needle felting to decorate the tail and make a shirt

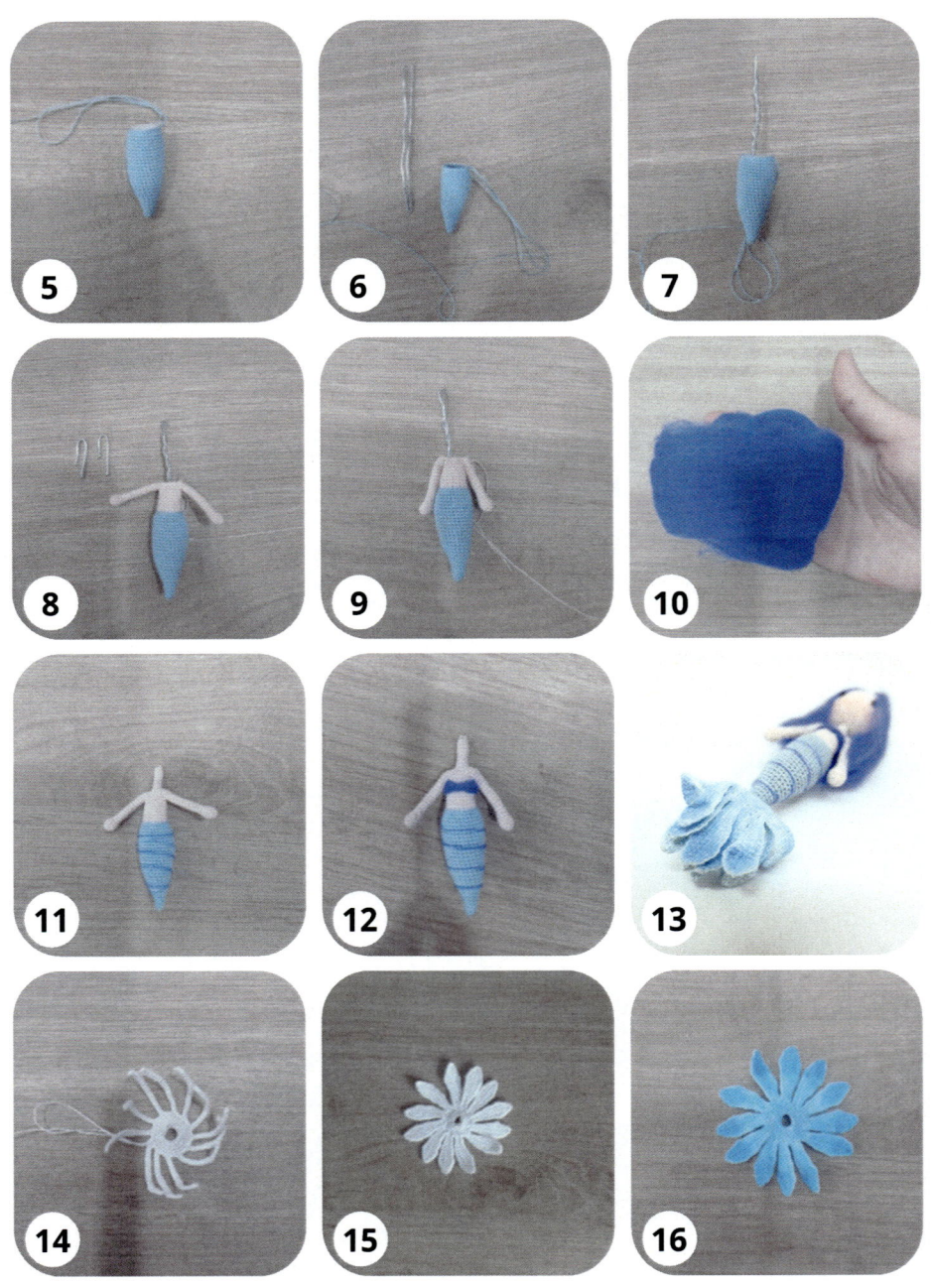

Flower
White color yarn
Rnd1. Mr 5sc
Rnd2. (2ch, 2dc, 2ch, slst)*5

Tail
White color yarn
Rnd1. 12ch, slst in the first chain to make a circle
Rnd2. 12inc [24]
Rnd3 – 4. 24sc [24]
Rnd5. (18ch, star in 2nd, 17slst, sc, slst)*12
Rnd6. (3sc, 3hdc, 4dc, 2tr, 2dc, hdc, 3sc in 1st, hdc, 2dc, 2tr, 4dc, 3hdc, 3sc)*12
Use watercolor to color the tail

Hair
I use needle felting for hair.

17   18   19

Chrysanthemums
Fairy Doll

Materials & Tools

Hook: 0,75mm

Yarn: YarnArt Canarias

Yarn color: skin, yellow, green, white

I use needle felting for hair - Brown color

Craft Wire: 1.5mm for body, 0.4mm for wings, petal

Cotton Stuffing

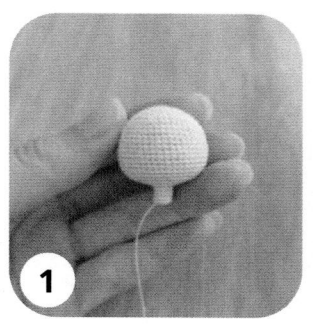

Head

Skin color yarn

Rnd1. Mr 6sc   [6]
Rnd2. 6inc [12]
Rnd3. (sc, inc)*6 [18]
Rnd4. (2sc, ins)*6 [24]
Rnd5. (3sc, ins)*6 [30]
Rnd6. (4sc, ins)*6 [36]
Rnd7. (5sc, ins)*6 [42]
Rnd8. (20sc, ins)*2 [44]

Rnd9 – 18. 44sc [44]
Rnd19. (20sc, dec)*2 [42]
Rnd20. (4sc, dec)*7 [35]
Rnd21. (3sc, dec)*7 [28]
Rnd22. (2sc, dec)*7 [21]
Rnd23. (sc, dec)*7 [14]
Rnd24. (sc, dec)*4, 2sc [10]
Rnd25. Blo 10sc [10]
Rnd26 – 28. 10sc [10]

Arms*2

Skin color yarn

Rnd1. Mr 6sc   [6]
Rnd2. (2inc, sc)*2   [10]
Rnd3 – 4. 10SC   [10]
Rnd5. (sc, dec)*3, sc   [7]
Rnd6 – 19. 7sc   [7]

 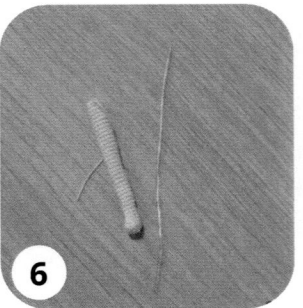 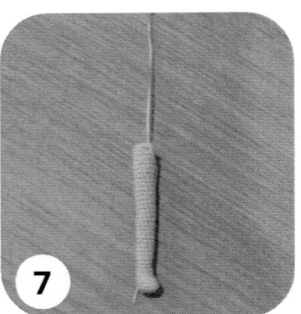

Legs*2
Skin color yarn

Rnd1. Ch5, turn: 3sc,3sc in 1st, 2sc, inc [10]

Rnd2. Inc, 2sc, 3inc, 2sc, 2inc [16]

Rnd3. Blo 16sc [16]

Rnd4. 3sc, 4dec, 5sc [12]

Rnd5. 2sc, 3dec, 4sc [9]

Rnd6 – 7. 9sc [9]

Rnd8. 8sc, inc [10]

Rnd9. 9sc, inc [11]

Rnd10 – 22. 11sc [11]

Rnd23. inc, 10sc [12]

Rnd24. inc, 11sc [13]

Rnd25 – 34. 13sc [13]

Rnd35. 4sc, inc, 8sc [14]

Put Craft Wire in leg

Body
Skin color yarn

Rnd37. Join 2 in legs and body into one piece

Continue crocheting on the right leg

Rnd36: ch2, 14sc on left leg, 2sc on ch2, 14 sc on right leg, 2sc on ch2 [32]

Rnd38 – 40. (7sc, inc)*4 [36]

Rnd41. (4sc, dec)*6 [30]

Rnd42. 30sc [30]

Rnd43. Blo (3sc, dec)*6 [24]

Rnd44. (dec, 10sc)*2 [22]

Rnd45 – 52. 22sc [22]

Join 2 arms and body into one piece.

Rnd53. 6sc on body, 3sc on body and arm, 8sc on body, 3sc on body and arm, 2sc on body [22]

Rnd54. 4sc, dec (on body), 4sc (on arm), dec, 4sc. dec (on body), 4sc (on arm), dec (on body) [20]

Rnd55. sc, (dec,sc)*6, sc [16]

Rnd56. sc, 6dec, sc [8]

Rnd57 – 64. 8sc [8]

Put Craft Wire in 2 arms

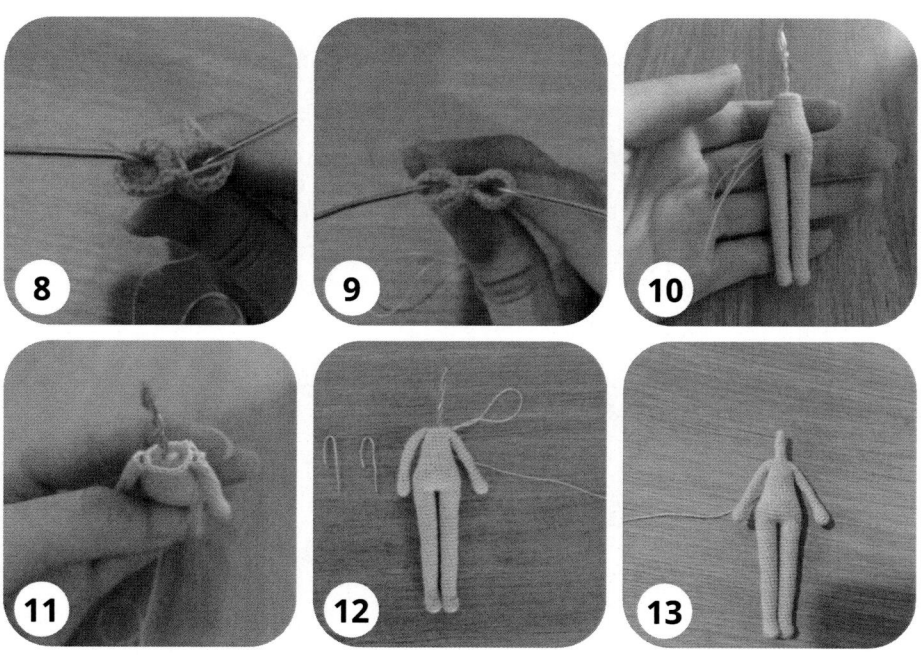

Dress

Green color yarn

Rnd1. 19ch, begin in second st, (2sc, 1inc)*6 [24]

Ch5, slst in 5th

Rnd2. (3sc, 1inc)*6, 1ch [30]

Rnd3. 3sc, 2hdc in 1st, 6dc, 1hdc, 8sc, 1hdc, 6dc, 2hdc in 1st, 3sc, 1ch [32]

Rnd4. Blo 3sc, inc, skip, inc, 6sc, inc, skip, Inc, 3sc, 1ch [20]

Rns5 – 7. 20dc [20]

Change to Yellow color yarn

Rnd8. Flo (2dc in 1st)*20 [40]

Rnd9. 40dc [40]

Rnd10. (dc, 2dc in 1st)*13, dc [53]

Rnd11. 53dc [53]

14

15

Petal *16

Yellow color yarn

Rnd1. 21ch, 19sc, 3sc in 1st, 19sc

Rnd2. 2sc, 2hdc, 2dc, 3hdc, sc, 3sc in 1st, sc, 3hdc, 12dc, 2hdc, 2sc

Put Craft Wire 0.4mm into petal

Rnd3. 1ch, 21sc, (1hdc, 2ch, 1hdc) in 1st , 21sc

Wings*2 (image 20)

Green color yarn

Rnd 1. 15ch, start in 2rd, sc, hdc, 9dc, hdc, sc, 3sc in 1st, sc,hdc, 9dc, hdc,sc

Put Craft Wire 0.4mm into wings

Rnd2. 29sc

Calyx (image 21)

Green color yarn

Rnd1. 26ch

Rnd2 – 3. 25sc

Rnd4. 5slst, (9ch, turn, 8slst, sc, hdc, dc, 2tr,dc, hdc,

(sc, 1ch,sc) in 1st , hdc, dc, 2tr, dc, hdc, sc, 4sc) *5

Flower

White color yarn

Rnd1. Mr 5sc

Rnd2. (2ch, 2dc, 2ch, slst)*5

Hair

I use needle felting for hair

Use a curling iron or iron to curl the hair

Rose Fairy Doll

Materials & Tools

Hook: 0,75mm

Yarn: YarnArt Canarias

Yarn color: skin, yellow, green, white

I use needle felting for hair

Craft Wire 1.5mm

Cotton Stuffing

Head

Skin color yarn

Rnd1. Mr 6sc   [6]

Rnd2. 6inc [12]

Rnd3. (sc, inc)*6 [18]

Rnd4. (2sc, ins)*6   [24]

Rnd5. (3sc, ins)*6 [30]

Rnd6. (4sc, ins)*6   [36]

Rnd7. (5sc, ins)*6 [42]

Rnd8. (20sc, ins)*2 [44]

Rnd9 – 18. 44sc [44]

Rnd19. (20sc, dec)*2 [42]

Rnd20. (4sc, dec)*7 [35]

Rnd21. (3sc, dec)*7 [28]

Rnd22. (2sc, dec)*7 [21]

Rnd23. (sc, dec)*7 [14]

Rnd24. (sc, dec)*4, 2sc [10]

Rnd25. Blo 10sc [10]

Rnd26 – 28. 10sc [10]

Arms*2

Skin color yarn

Rnd1. Mr 6sc   [6]

Rnd2. (2inc, sc)*2   [10]

Rnd3 – 4. 10SC   [10]

Rnd5. (sc, dec)*3, sc   [7]

Rnd6 – 19. 7sc   [7]

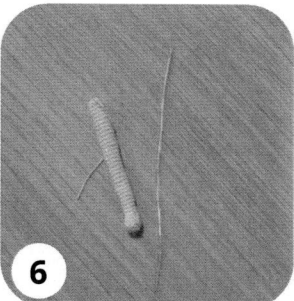
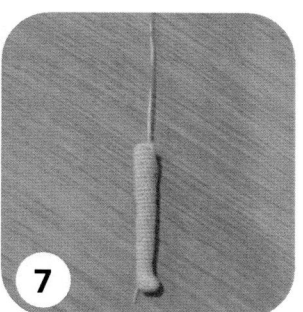

5 **6** **7**

Legs*2
Skin color yarn
Rnd1. Ch5, turn: 3sc,3sc in 1st, 2sc, inc [10]

Rnd2. Inc, 2sc, 3inc, 2sc, 2inc [16]

Rnd3. Blo 16sc [16]

Rnd4. 3sc, 4dec, 5sc [12]

Rnd5. 2sc, 3dec, 4sc [9]

Rnd6 – 7. 9sc [9]

Rnd8. 8sc, inc [10]

Rnd9. 9sc, inc [11]

Rnd10 – 22. 11sc [11]

Rnd23. inc, 10sc [12]

Rnd24. inc, 11sc [13]

Rnd25 – 34. 13sc [13]

Rnd35. 4sc, inc, 8sc [14]

Put Craft Wire into leg

Body
Skin color yarn
Rnd37. Join 2 in legs and body into one piece

Continue crocheting on the right leg

Rnd36: ch2, 14sc on left leg, 2sc on ch2, 14 sc on right leg, 2sc on ch2 [32]

Rnd38 – 40. (7sc, inc)*4 [36]

Rnd41. (4sc, dec)*6 [30]

Rnd42. 30sc [30]

Rnd43. Blo (3sc, dec)*6 [24]

Rnd44. (dec, 10sc)*2 [22]

Rnd45 – 52. 22sc [22]

Join 2 arms and body into one piece.

Rnd53. 6sc on body, 3sc on body and arm, 8sc on body, 3sc on body and arm, 2sc on body [22]

Rnd54. 4sc, dec (on body), 4sc (on arm), dec, 4sc. dec (on body), 4sc (on arm), dec (on body) [20]

Rnd55. sc, (dec,sc)*6, sc [16]

Rnd56. sc, 6dec, sc [8]

Rnd57 – 64. 8sc [8]

Put Craft Wire in 2 arms

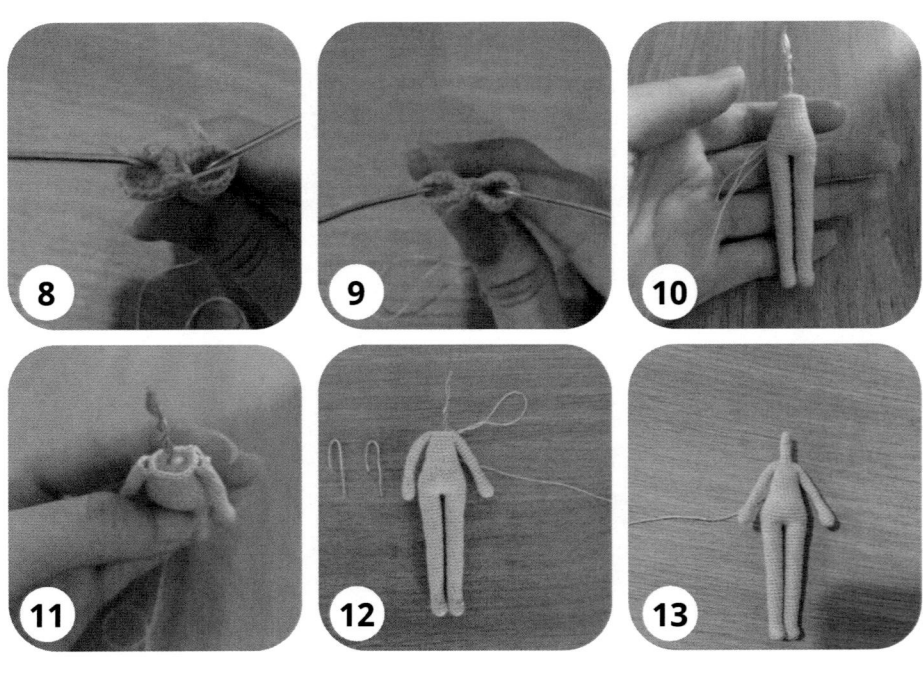

27

Dress

Light pink color yarn

Rnd1. 19ch, begin in second st, (2sc, 1inc)*6 [24]

Ch5, slst in 5th

Rnd2. (3sc, 1inc)*6, 1ch [30]

Rnd3. 3sc, 2hdc in 1st, 6dc, 1hdc, 8sc, 1hdc, 6dc,, 2hdc in 1st, 3sc, 1ch [32]

Rnd4. Blo 3sc, inc, skip, inc, 6sc, inc, skip, Inc, 3sc, 1ch [20]

Rnd5 – 7. 20dc [20]

Change to pink color yarn

Rnd8. Flo (2dc in 1st)*20 [40]

Rnd9. 40dc [40]

Rnd10. (dc, 2dc in 1st)*13, dc [53]

Rnd11 – 12. 53dc [53]

Petal

Medium*8(image 16)

Rnd1. Mr 5sc [5]

Rnd2. 5inc [10]

Rnd3. (sc, inc)*5 [15]

Rnd4. (2sc, inc)*5 [20]

Rnd5. (3sc, inc)*5 [25]

Rnd6. (4sc, inc)*5 [30]

Rnd7. (5sc, inc)*5 [35]

Rnd8. 6sc, (2hdc in 1st, 6hdc)*3, 2hdc in 1st, 7sc

Rnd9. 7dc, (2dc in 1st)*12, (2dc in 1st, ch1, 2dc in 1st), (2dc in 1st)*12, 7dc

Small size*8(image 17)

Rnd1. Mr 5sc   [5]

Rnd2. 5inc   [10]

Rnd3. (sc, inc)*5 [15]

Rnd4. (2sc, inc)*5   [20]

Rnd5. (3sc, inc)*5   [25]

Rnd6. (4sc, inc)*5   [30]

Rnd7. 11sc, 2hdc in 1st, 2hdc, 2hdc in 1st, 2hdc, 2hdc in 1st, 12sc

Rnd8. 11dc, (2dc in 1st)*10, 12dc

Big size*4(image 18)

Pink color yarn

Rnd1. Mr 5sc [5]

Rnd2. 5inc   [10]

Rnd3. (sc, inc)*5 [15]

Rnd4. (2sc, inc)*5 [20]

Rnd5. (3sc, inc)*5 [25]

Rnd6. (4sc, inc)*5 [30]

Rnd7. (5sc, inc)*5 [35]

Rnd8. (sc, inc)*5 [40]

Rnd9. 7hdc, (2hdc in 1st 3hdc)*6, 2hdc in 1st, 8hdc

Rnd10. 7dc, (2dc in 1st)*16, (2dc in 1st, ch2, 2dc in 1st), (2dc in 1st)*16, 7dc

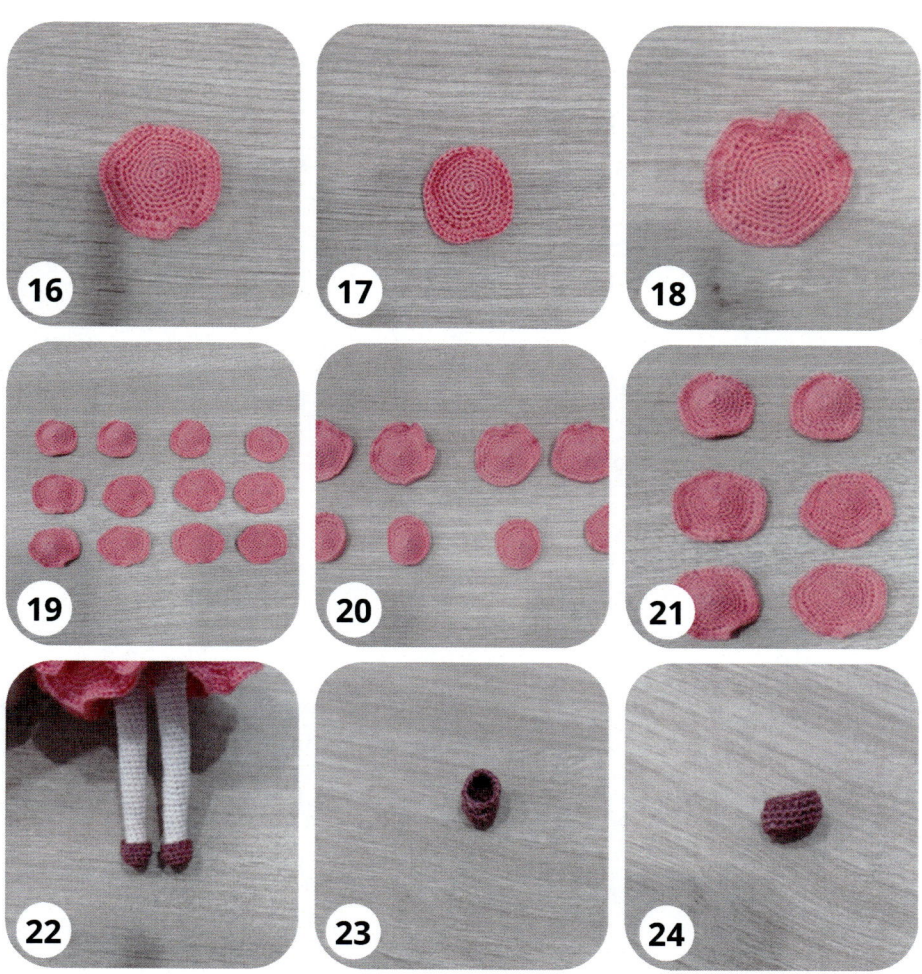

Shoes

Rnd1. Ch6, start to 2st, 4sc, 3sc in 1st, 3sc, ínc [12]
Rnd2. inc, 3sc, 3inc, 3sc, 2inc [18]
Rnd3. Blo, 18sc [18]
Rnd4. 18sc [18]
Rnd5. 4sc,4dec, 6sc, slst

Hair

I use needle felting for hair.

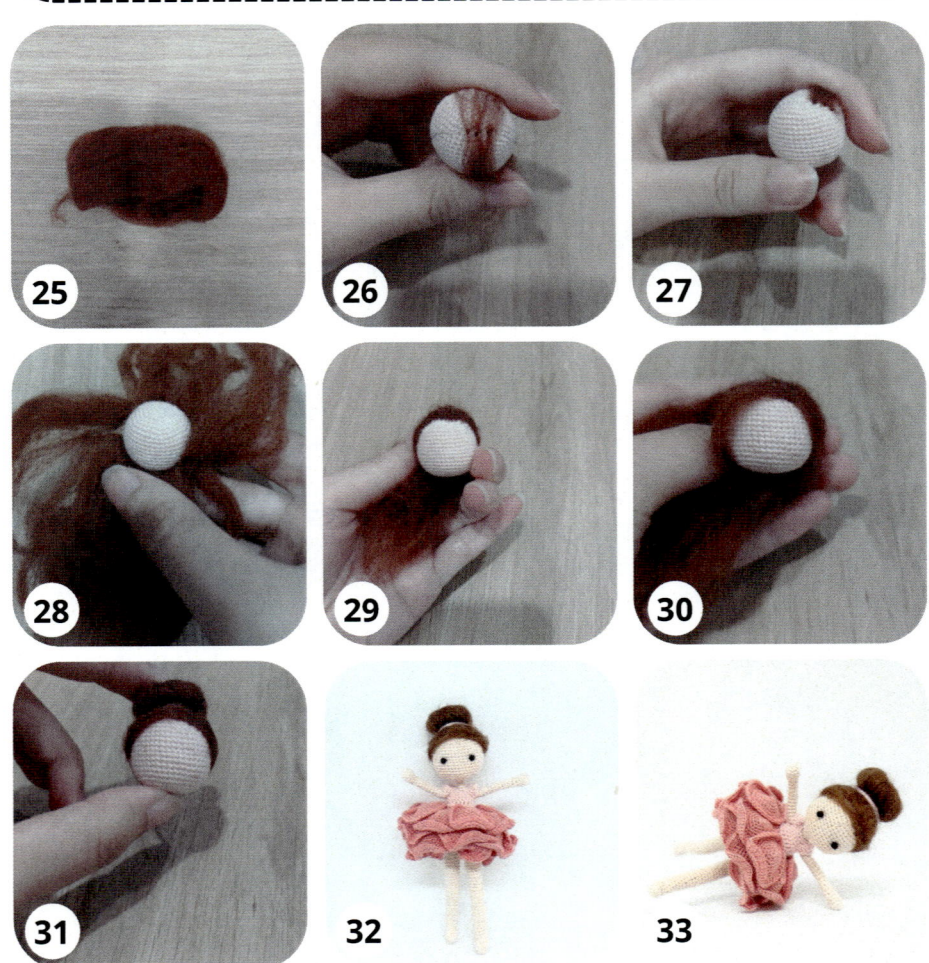

25

26

27

28

29

30

31

32

33

Pink Rose Fairy Doll

Materials & Tools

Hook: 0,75mm

Yarn: YarnArt Canarias

Yarn color: skin, green, white, pink, light pink

I use needle felting for hair

Craft Wire 1.5mm for body, 0.4mm for wings and petals

Cotton Stuffing

Head
Skin color yarn

Rnd1. Mr 6sc   [6]
Rnd2. 6inc [12]
Rnd3. (sc, inc)*6 [18]
Rnd4. (2sc, ins)*6   [24]
Rnd5. (3sc, ins)*6 [30]
Rnd6. (4sc, ins)*6   [36]
Rnd7. (5sc, ins)*6 [42]
Rnd8. (20sc, ins)*2 [44]

Rnd9 – 18. 44sc [44]
Rnd19. (20sc, dec)*2 [42]
Rnd20. (4sc, dec)*7 [35]
Rnd21. (3sc, dec)*7 [28]
Rnd22. (2sc, dec)*7 [21]
Rnd23. (sc, dec)*7 [14]
Rnd24. (sc, dec)*4, 2sc [10]
Rnd25. Blo 10sc [10]
Rnd26 – 28. 10sc [10]

Arms*2
Skin color yarn

Rnd1. Mr 6sc   [6]
Rnd2. (2inc, sc)*2   [10]
Rnd3 – 4. 10SC   [10]
Rnd5. (sc, dec)*3, sc   [7]
Rnd6 – 19. 7sc   [7]

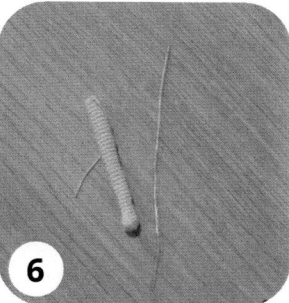
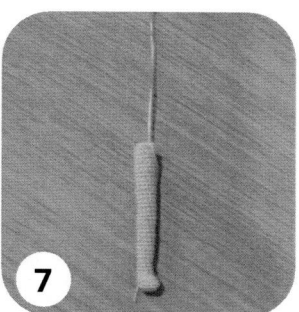

Legs*2
Skin color yarn

Rnd1. Ch5, turn: 3sc,3sc in 1st, 2sc, inc [10]

Rnd2. Inc, 2sc, 3inc, 2sc, 2inc [16]

Rnd3. Blo 16sc [16]

Rnd4. 3sc, 4dec, 5sc [12]

Rnd5. 2sc, 3dec, 4sc [9]

Rnd6 – 7. 9sc [9]

Rnd8. 8sc, inc [10]

Rnd9. 9sc, inc [11]

Rnd10 – 22. 11sc [11]

Rnd23. inc, 10sc [12]

Rnd24. inc, 11sc [13]

Rnd25 – 34. 13sc [13]

Rnd35. 4sc, inc, 8sc [14]

Put Craft Wire into leg

Body
Skin color yarn

Rnd37. Join 2 in legs and body into one piece

Continue crocheting on the right leg

Rnd36: ch2, 14sc on left leg, 2sc on ch2, 14 sc on right leg, 2sc on ch2 [32]

Rnd38 – 40. (7sc, inc)*4 [36]

Rnd41. (4sc, dec)*6 [30]

Rnd42. 30sc [30]

Rnd43. Blo (3sc, dec)*6 [24]

Rnd44. (dec, 10sc)*2 [22]

Rnd45 – 52. 22sc [22]

Join 2 arms and body into one piece.

Rnd53. 6sc on body, 3sc on body and arm, 8sc on body, 3sc on body and arm, 2sc on body [22]

Rnd54. 4sc, dec (on body), 4sc (on arm), dec, 4sc. dec (on body), 4sc (on arm), dec (on body) [20]

Rnd55. sc, (dec,sc)*6, sc [16]

Rnd56. sc, 6dec, sc [8]

Rnd57 – 64. 8sc [8]

Put Craft Wire in 2 arms

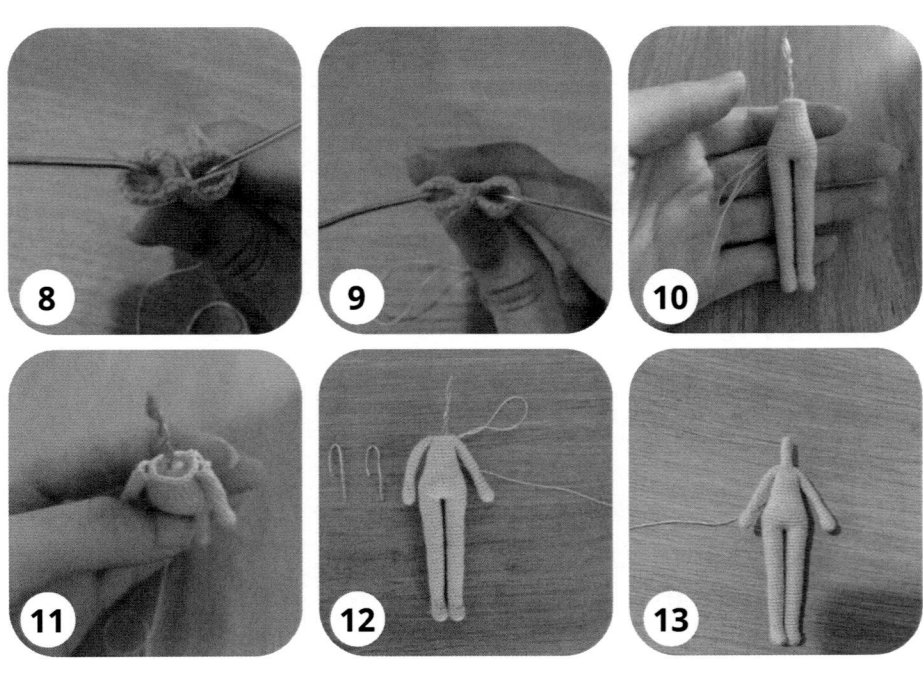

Dress

Pink color yarn

Rnd1. 21ch, start in 2rd, 20sc [20]

Rnd2. 20dc [20]

Rnd3.20sc [20]

Rnd4. 20dc [20]

Rnd5. 20sc [20]

Change to light pink color yarn.

Rnd8. Flo (2dc in 1st)*20 [40]

Rnd9. 40dc [40]

Rnd10. (dc, 2dc in 1st)*13, dc [53]

Rnd11. 53dc [53]

Petal

Small size*7

Light pink color yarn.

Rnd1. 14ch, start in 2nd, 2sc, 2hdc, 8dc, 7dc in 1st, 8dc, 2hdc, 2sc

Rnd2. 4sc, 3hdc, 6dc, (2dc in 1st)*5, 6dc, 3hdc, 4sc

Put Craft Wire (0,4mm)

Rnd3. 4sc, 3hdc, 3dc, (2dc in 1st)*4, (dc, slst), (slst, ch, hdc), (2dc in 1st)*4, (dc, slst), (slst,ch, hdc), (2dc in 1st)*4, 3dc. 3hdc, 4sc, slst

Big size*4

Light pink color yarn.

Rnd1. 17ch, start in 2nd, 3sc, 3hdc, 9dc,

7dc in 1st, 9dc, 3hdc, 3sc

Rnd2. 5sc, 3hdc, 6dc, (2dc in 1st)*9 , 6dc, 3hdc, 5sc

Put Craft Wire (0,4mm)

Rnd3. 4sc, 6hdc, 5dc(2dc in 1st)*4, (dc, slst), (slst, ch, hdc), (2dc in 1st)*4, (dc, slst), (slst,ch, hdc), (2dc in 1st)*4, 5dc. 6hdc, 4sc, slst

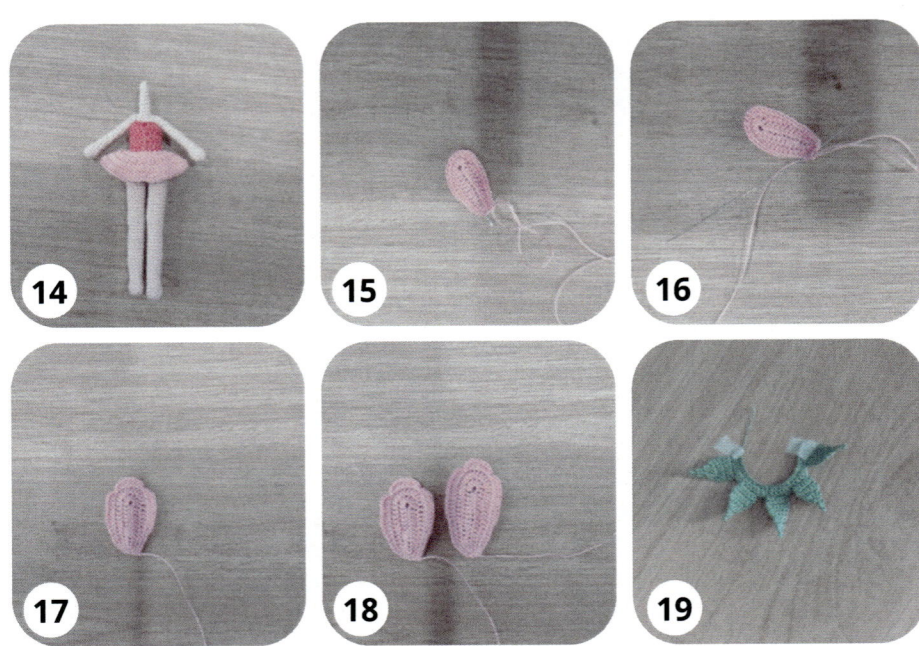

Calyx

Green color yarn

Rnd1. 31ch, start in 2nd, 30sc
Rnd2. Ch, 30hdc
Rnd3. 6sc, ch1, turn
Rnd4. (inc, sc)*2, ch1, turn
Rnd5 – 6. 6sc, ch1, turn
Rnd7. Dec, 4sc, ch1, turn

Rnd8. Dec, 3sc, ch1, turn
Rnd9. Dec, 2sc, ch1, turn
Rnd10. Dec, sc, ch1, turn
Rnd11. 2sc, ch1, turn
Rnd12. Dec, ch1, turn
Rnd13. Hdc, 2ch, cut the yarn
Repeat Rnd4 – 13 for remaining
4 part

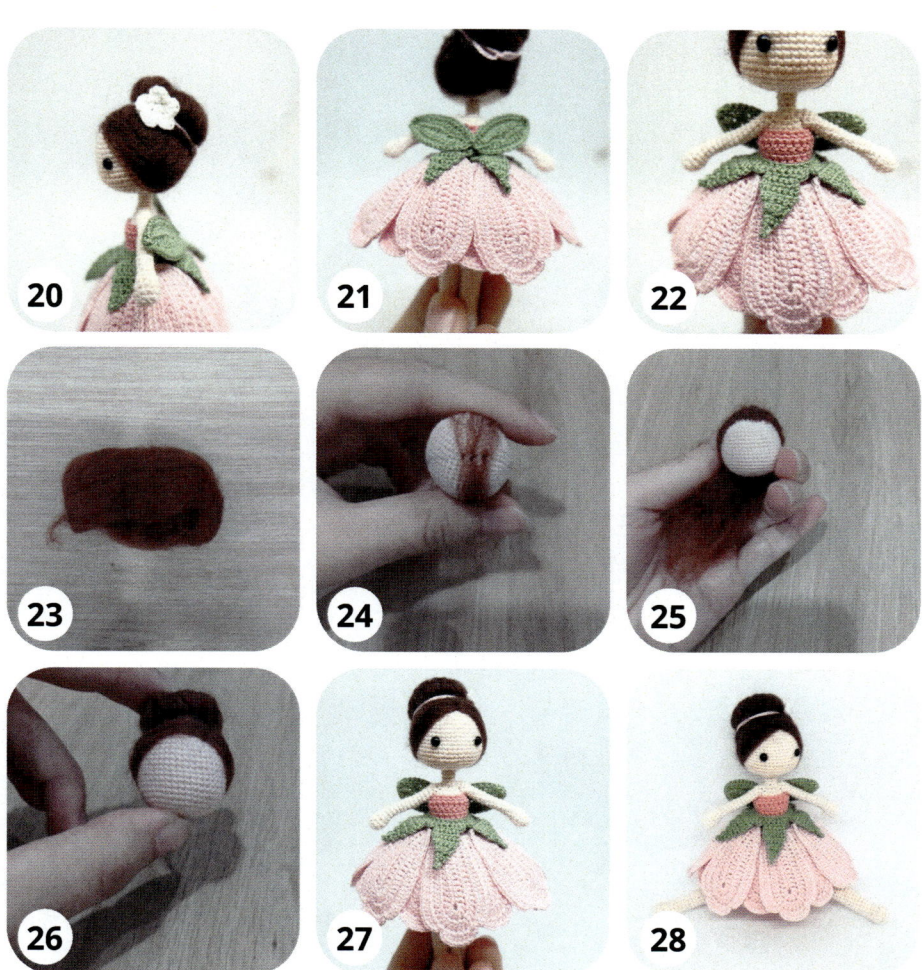

Wings*2
Green color yarn
Rnd1. 15ch, start in 2rd, sc, hdc, 9dc, hdc, sc, 3sc in 1st, sc, hdc, 9dc, hdc,sc
Put craft wire into wings
Rnd2. 29sc

Flower
White color yarn
Rnd1. Mr 5sc
Rnd2. (2ch, 2dc, 2ch, slst)*5
Use craft wire to make hair pins and then attach flowers

Hair
Use needle felting for hair.

38

Forest Fairy Doll

Materials & Tools

Hook: 0,75mm

Yarn: YarnArt Canarias

Yarn color: skin, green, white, purple

I use needle felting for hair

Craft Wire 1.5mm for body, 0.4mm for wings and petals

Cotton Stuffing

Head

Skin color yarn

Rnd1. Mr 6sc   [6]

Rnd2. 6inc [12]

Rnd3. (sc, inc)*6 [18]

Rnd4. (2sc, ins)*6 [24]

Rnd5. (3sc, ins)*6 [30]

Rnd6. (4sc, ins)*6 [36]

Rnd7. (5sc, ins)*6 [42]

Rnd8. (20sc, ins)*2 [44]

Rnd9 – 18. 44sc [44]

Rnd19. (20sc, dec)*2 [42]

Rnd20. (4sc, dec)*7 [35]

Rnd21. (3sc, dec)*7 [28]

Rnd22. (2sc, dec)*7 [21]

Rnd23. (sc, dec)*7 [14]

Rnd24. (sc, dec)*4, 2sc [10]

Rnd25. Blo 10sc [10]

Rnd26 – 28. 10sc [10]

Arms*2

Skin color yarn

Rnd1. Mr 6sc   [6]

Rnd2. (2inc, sc)*2 [10]

Rnd3 – 4. 10SC   [10]

Rnd5. (sc, dec)*3, sc   [7]

Rnd6 – 19. 7sc   [7]

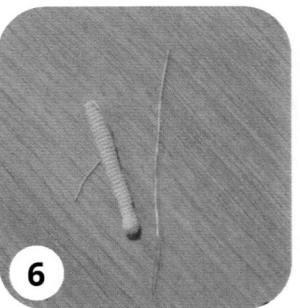
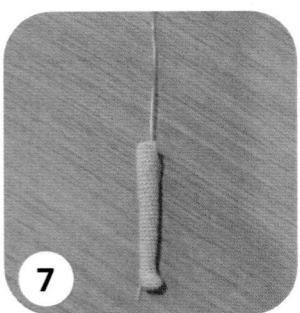

Legs*2
Skin color yarn

Rnd1. Ch5, turn: 3sc,3sc in 1st, 2sc, inc [10]

Rnd2. Inc, 2sc, 3inc, 2sc, 2inc [16]

Rnd3. Blo 16sc [16]

Rnd4. 3sc, 4dec, 5sc [12]

Rnd5. 2sc, 3dec, 4sc [9]

Rnd6 – 7. 9sc [9]

Rnd8. 8sc, inc [10]

Rnd9. 9sc, inc [11]

Rnd10 – 22. 11sc [11]

Rnd23. inc, 10sc [12]

Rnd24. inc, 11sc [13]

Rnd25 – 34. 13sc [13]

Rnd35. 4sc, inc, 8sc [14]

Put Craft Wire into leg

Body
Skin color yarn

Rnd37. Join 2 in legs and body into one piece

Continue crocheting on the right leg

Rnd36: ch2, 14sc on left leg, 2sc on ch2, 14 sc on right leg, 2sc on ch2 [32]

Rnd38 – 40. (7sc, inc)*4 [36]

Rnd41. (4sc, dec)*6 [30]

Rnd42. 30sc [30]

Rnd43. Blo (3sc, dec)*6 [24]

Rnd44. (dec, 10sc)*2 [22]

Rnd45 – 52. 22sc [22]

Join 2 arms and body into one piece.

Rnd53. 6sc on body, 3sc on body and arm, 8sc on body, 3sc on body and arm, 2sc on body [22]

Rnd54. 4sc, dec (on body), 4sc (on arm), dec, 4sc. dec (on body), 4sc (on arm), dec (on body) [20]

Rnd55. sc, (dec,sc)*6, sc [16]

Rnd56. sc, 6dec, sc [8]

Rnd57 – 64. 8sc [8]

Put Craft Wire in 2 arms

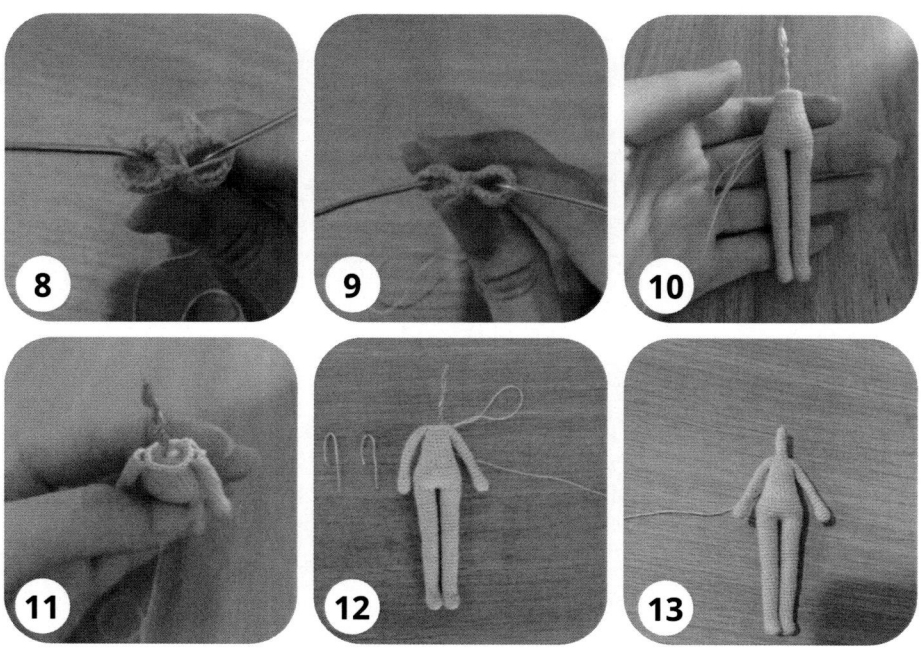

Dress

Purple color yarn
Rnd1. 25ch, start in 6th, 20sc [20]
Rnd2 – 4. 20dc [20]
Change to green color yarn
Rnd5. (2dc in 1st)*20 [40]
Rnd9 – 12. 40dc [40]

Leaves

Make a dress *8
Green Color Yarn
Rnd1. 40ch, start in 2nd, 2sc, 2hdc, 30dc, 2hdc, 2sc, 3sc in 1st ,
2sc, 2hdc, 30dc, 2hdc, 2sc
Rnd2. 2sc, 2hdc, 30dc, 2hdc, 3sc, (sc, 1ch, sc) , 3sc, 2hdc, 30dc,
2hdc, 2sc
Rnd3. 9sc, 2hdc, 22dc, 2hdc, 5sc, 2ch, 5sc, 2hdc, 22dc, 2hdc, 9sc

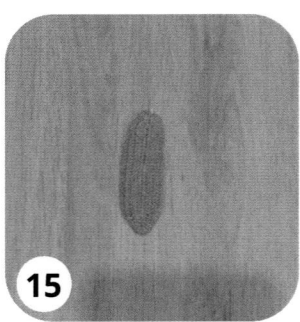

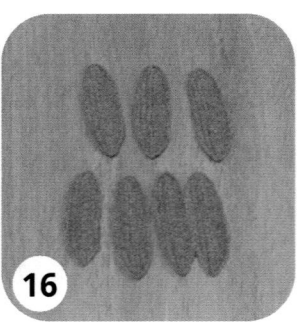

Wing

Green Color Yarn

Rnd1. 10ch, start in 2nd , turn, 9sc

Rnd2. 4ch, start in 2nd , turn, 9sc

Rnd3. Turn, 9sc

Rnd4. 4ch, start in 2nd , turn, 9sc

Rnd5. Turn, 9sc

Rnd6. 4ch, start in 2nd , turn, 9sc

Rnd7. Turn, 9sc

Rnd8. 4ch, start in 2nd , turn, 9sc

Rnd9. Turn,6sc

Rnd10. Turn, 9sc (connect with 3 stich in Rnd7)

Rnd11. Turn,6sc

Rnd12. Turn, 9sc (connect with 3 stich in Rnd5)

Rnd13. Turn,6sc

Rnd14. Turn, 9sc (connect with 3 stich in Rnd3)

Rnd15. Turn,6sc

Rnd16. Turn, 9sc (connect with 3 stich in Rnd1)

18   19   20

Flower

Purple color yarn *15
Mr (2ch, 2dc, 2ch, slst)*5
White color yarn*1
Rnd1. Mr 5sc
Rnd2. (2ch, 2dc, 2ch, slst)*5

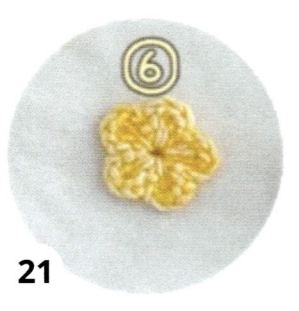

21

22

23

Hair
Use needle felting for hair.

24

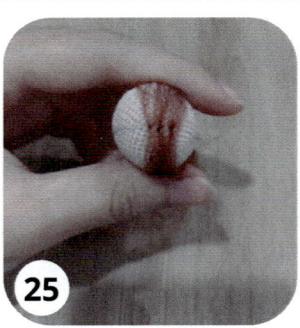

25

26

27

28

29

Daisy Fairy Doll

Materials & Tools

Hook: 0,75mm

Yarn: YarnArt Canarias

Yarn color: skin, white, yellow

I use needle felting for hair

Craft Wire 1.5mm for body, 0.4mm for wings and petals

Cotton Stuffing

Head

Skin color yarn

Rnd1. Mr 6sc   [6]

Rnd2. 6inc [12]

Rnd3. (sc, inc)*6 [18]

Rnd4. (2sc, ins)*6   [24]

Rnd5. (3sc, ins)*6 [30]

Rnd6. (4sc, ins)*6   [36]

Rnd7. (5sc, ins)*6 [42]

Rnd8. (20sc, ins)*2 [44]

Rnd9 – 18. 44sc [44]

Rnd19. (20sc, dec)*2 [42]

Rnd20. (4sc, dec)*7 [35]

Rnd21. (3sc, dec)*7 [28]

Rnd22. (2sc, dec)*7 [21]

Rnd23. (sc, dec)*7 [14]

Rnd24. (sc, dec)*4, 2sc [10]

Rnd25. Blo 10sc [10]

Rnd26 – 28. 10sc [10]

Arms*2

Skin color yarn

Rnd1. Mr 6sc   [6]

Rnd2. (2inc, sc)*2   [10]

Rnd3 – 4. 10SC   [10]

Rnd5. (sc, dec)*3, sc   [7]

Rnd6 – 19. 7sc   [7]

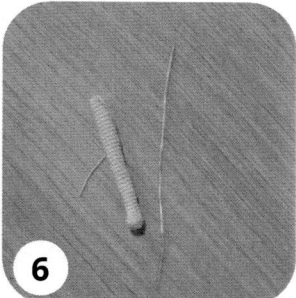
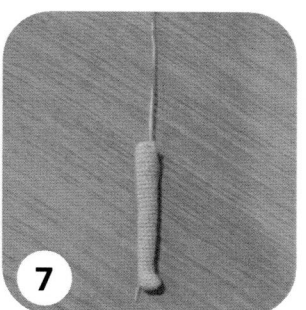

Legs*2
Skin color yarn

Rnd1. Ch5, turn: 3sc,3sc in 1st, 2sc, inc [10]

Rnd2. Inc, 2sc, 3inc, 2sc, 2inc [16]

Rnd3. Blo 16sc [16]

Rnd4. 3sc, 4dec, 5sc [12]

Rnd5. 2sc, 3dec, 4sc [9]

Rnd6 – 7. 9sc [9]

Rnd8. 8sc, inc [10]

Rnd9. 9sc, inc [11]

Rnd10 – 22. 11sc [11]

Rnd23. inc, 10sc [12]

Rnd24. inc, 11sc [13]

Rnd25 – 34. 13sc [13]

Rnd35. 4sc, inc, 8sc [14]

Put Craft Wire into leg

Body
Skin color yarn

Rnd37. Join 2 in legs and body into one piece

Continue crocheting on the right leg

Rnd36: ch2, 14sc on left leg, 2sc on ch2, 14 sc on right leg, 2sc on ch2 [32]

Rnd38 – 40. (7sc, inc)*4 [36]

Rnd41. (4sc, dec)*6 [30]

Rnd42. 30sc [30]

Rnd43. Blo (3sc, dec)*6 [24]

Rnd44. (dec, 10sc)*2 [22]

Rnd45 – 52. 22sc [22]

Join 2 arms and body into one piece.

Rnd53. 6sc on body, 3sc on body and arm, 8sc on body, 3sc on body and arm, 2sc on body [22]

Rnd54. 4sc, dec (on body), 4sc (on arm), dec, 4sc. dec (on body), 4sc (on arm), dec (on body) [20]

Rnd55. sc, (dec,sc)*6, sc [16]

Rnd56. sc, 6dec, sc [8]

Rnd57 – 64. 8sc [8]

Put Craft Wire in 2 arms

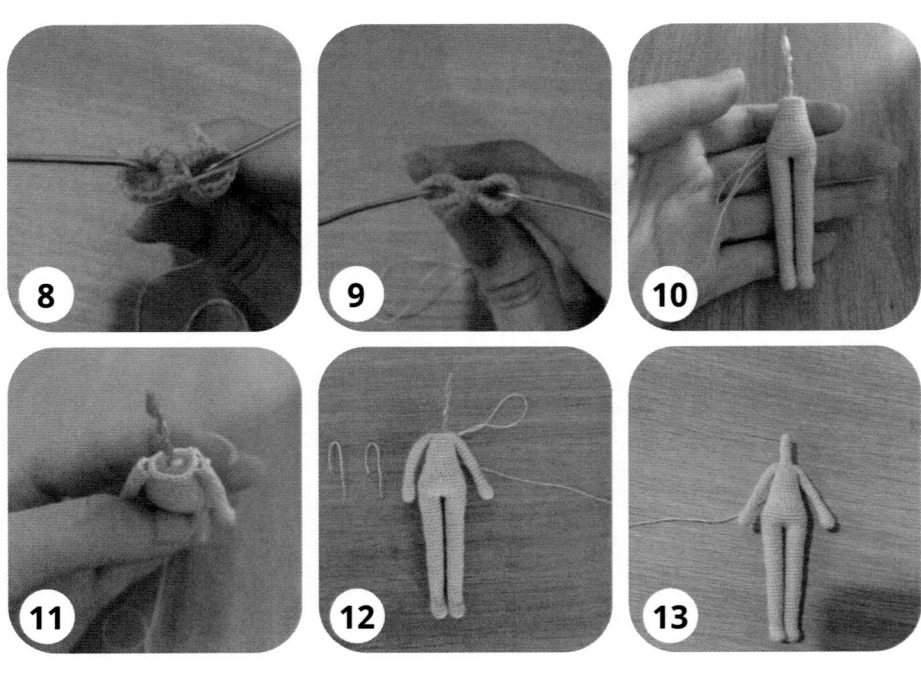

Dress

Yellow color yarn

Rnd1. 21ch, start in 2rd, 20sc [20]

Rnd2. 20dc [20]

Rnd3.20sc [20]

Rnd4. 20dc [20]

Rnd5. 20sc [20]

Change to white color yarn

Rnd8. Flo (2dc in 1st)*20 [40]

Rnd9. 40dc [40]

Rnd10. (dc, 2dc in 1st)*13, dc [53]

Rnd11. 53dc [53]

Petal

White color yarn

Small size*10

Rnd1: 13ch, start in 2nd , 11sc, 2slst,11sc

Rnd2: 2sc, 2hdc, 6dc, hdc, (sc, 2ch, sc), hdc, 6dc, 2hdc, 2sc

Big size*25

Rnd1: 15ch, start in 2nd , 13sc, 2slst, 13sc

Rnd2: 2sc, 2hdc, 8dc, hdc, (sc, 2ch, sc), hdc, 8dc, 2hdc, 2sc

14

15

16

Wings

Yellow color yarn

Small size *2

Rnd1: 10ch, start in 2nd , 8sc, 2slst,8sc

Put in craft ware 0,4mm

Rnd2: 2sc, 2hdc, 4dc, hdc, (sc, 2ch, sc), hdc, 4dc, 2hdc, 2sc

Big size *2

Rnd1: 15ch, start in 2nd , 13sc, 2slst,13sc

Put in craft ware

Rnd2: 2sc, 2hdc, 8dc, hdc, (sc, 2ch, sc), hdc, 8dc, 2hdc, 2sc

Flower

White color yarn

Rnd1. Mr 5sc

Rnd2. (2ch, 2dc, 2ch, slst)*5

Hair

Use needle felting for hair.

Made in the USA
Monee, IL
21 August 2024

64236435R00033